Early Learning
BULLETIN BOARDS
Includes Patterns, Projects and Activities

by
Vanessa Filkins

Cover by Vanessa Filkins

Copyright © Good Apple, Inc., 1990

ISBN No. 0-86653-529-2

Printing No. 98765

Good Apple, Inc.
1204 Buchanan, Box 299
Carthage, IL 62321-0299

The purchase of this book entitles the buyer to reproduce student activity pages for classroom use only. Any other use requires the written permission of Good Apple, Inc.

All rights reserved. Printed in the United States of America.

Table of Contents

Quick and Easy Border Tips

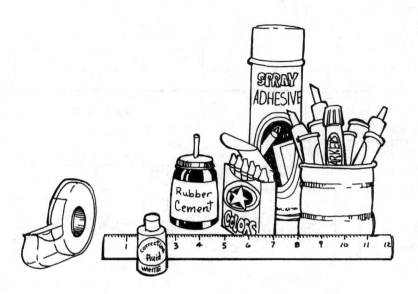

Equipment:

copy machine
ruler
scissors
colored markers or crayons
transparent tape
rubber cement or spray adhesive
Liquid Paper correction fluid

How To:

1. Choose a design, measure area to be covered and calculate number of panels needed.

Conserve Paper:

After making two or three photocopies of design needed, trim and add adhesive to the back, using rubber cement or spray adhesive. Now gang them onto one sheet of paper. (See illustration.)

Clean Copies:

Sometimes the cut lines will photocopy as black lines. To solve this problem, make one photocopy and white out the cut lines and unwanted flaws. Use this as your master copy.

Sizes:

If your photocopy machine is equipped, enlarge or reduce the design for a variety of sizes to suit your special needs.

2. Trim borders and color with bright-colored markers or crayons.

Copyright © 1990, Good Apple, Inc.

GA1141

3. Place borders end to end, taping together on back side until desired length is achieved. (See illustration.)

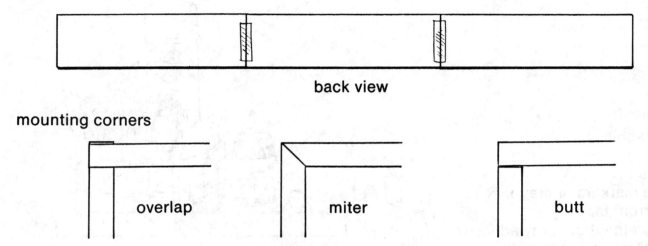

back view

mounting corners

overlap   miter   butt

4. **3-D Pop-Up Borders:**
Make extra photocopies of border. Color and cut out individual designs, and glue a small loop tab to the back of each one. When the glue is dry, glue tab directly over same design on border strip. (See illustration.)

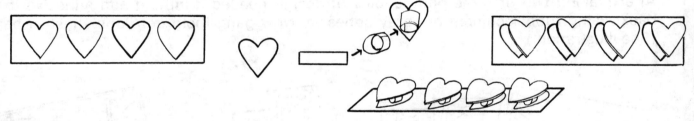

Hints:
- For really quick borders use colored stock paper when making photocopies to eliminate hand coloring.

- Mix and match two or more borders.

- After coloring the design, laminate with clear Con-Tact paper for durability. Use over and over.

Other Hints:
Turn your trimming project into a fun classroom or school activity. Let students color borders individually or in small groups.

Cut out for use as name tags.

Make your own flash cards.

Frame or highlight student papers.

Make bookmarks by cutting design to desired length. Next color, laminate, punch hole and add yarn tassel.

Make holiday ornaments and mobiles. Cut designs apart and glue to lightweight cardboard. Next color or decorate with sequins, glitter, felt scraps or cotton batting. Punch small hole and add string.

Copyright © 1990, Good Apple, Inc.

GA1141

Welcome Back to School

Materials:

markers
construction paper
cardboard toilet tissue tube
glue

transparent tape
crayons
markers
yarn

Welcome your students back with a welcome-back-to-school bulletin board that they personalize. Start by covering the upper two thirds of your board with light-blue paper. Cover the remaining upper half of exposed board with green paper in the shape of hills and the bottom with grey construction paper to represent a road. Enlarge and reproduce the school bus pattern onto yellow construction paper or poster board. Using the above illustration as a guide, cut out a large trunk and treetop from brown and green construction paper. Spray paint Styrofoam packing peanuts green and glue to top of tree. Using a black marker, add bark detail to tree trunk. Finally, enlarge and reproduce banner to desired size and make airplane, following directions on craft page 4. Let each child decorate an oval piece of construction paper with a self-portrait. Help him add his name and position the portrait on school bus.

Copyright © 1990, Good Apple, Inc.

1

GA1141

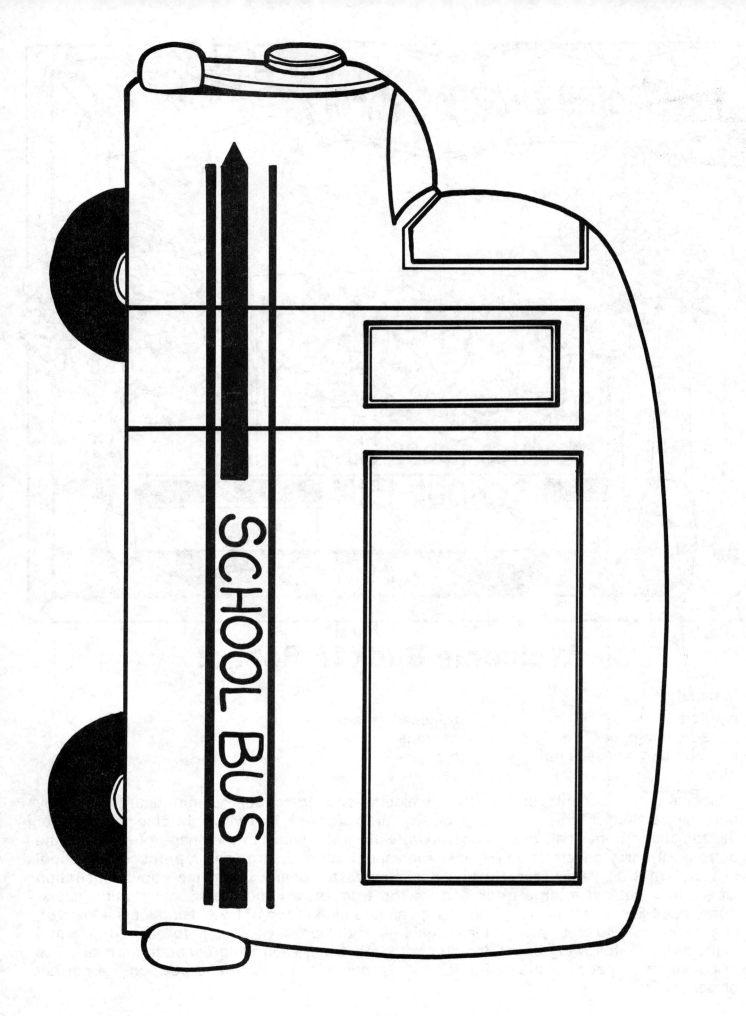

SCHOOL BUS

Copyright © 1990, Good Apple, Inc.

2

GA1141

pilot

wing

propeller

tail

motor

Welcome Back to School

Copyright © 1990, Good Apple, Inc.

3

GA1141

Welcome Back to School
Crafts

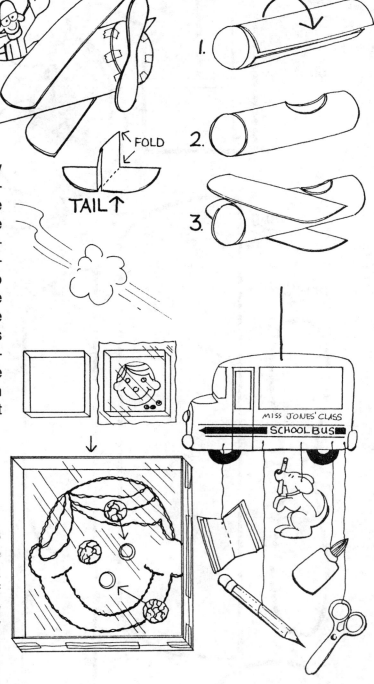

Airplane

To make your airplane, first glue yellow construction paper on tube. (See illustration 1.) For the plane's cockpit cut a hole in the tube as in illustration 2. To make the wings, glue two sheets of paper together, making sure one sheet is completely covered with glue. Let dry. Next cut two wings out of that piece of paper using the wing pattern provided on page 3 and glue to plane. (See illustration 3.) Using patterns provided, cut out a tail, motor and propeller. Tape motor to tube. Fold and glue tail in position. Finally glue propeller on plane and reproduce, color and glue pilot in cockpit.

Put on a Happy Face

Put a happy face on your students' faces again and again with this easy-to-make puzzle. Glue or tape open end of box closed. Now cut off one large flat side of box so it forms a tray. Let each child draw self-portrait on the inside bottom of his/her tray or use self-portrait from bulletin board glued to the box bottom. Next, with the help of the teacher, punch holes through the eyes and nose. Put three marbles in each box, or make balls out of aluminum foil slightly larger than the pencil holes in box. Finally cover the top of the tray with plastic wrap and tape to sides of box. Now you are ready to play by wiggling the box so the balls fall into the holes.

Welcome Back Mobile

To make this mobile, reproduce school bus, banner and puppy onto tagboard. Color with markers. Using several folded rectangle-shaped pieces of construction paper, form small books. Glue the binding. Hang banner, bus and school items from string as in illustration.

Copyright © 1990, Good Apple, Inc.

GA1141

Welcome to My Class

Materials:

markers
construction paper
scissors

Welcome your students back to class with this cheerful bulletin board that includes a name tag for everyone. Cover the board with green construction paper. Reproduce and color enough border pattern to cover border area. Enlarge and color title and other school illustrations to desired size, leaving enough remaining space to hold name tags. Reproduce and attach one name tag for each child to the completed bulletin board. After each child receives his/her name tag, use the board to display classwork.

Copyright © 1990, Good Apple, Inc.

GA1141

Copyright © 1990, Good Apple, Inc.

6

GA1141

Copyright © 1990, Good Apple, Inc.

7

GA1141

Copyright © 1990, Good Apple, Inc.

8

GA1141

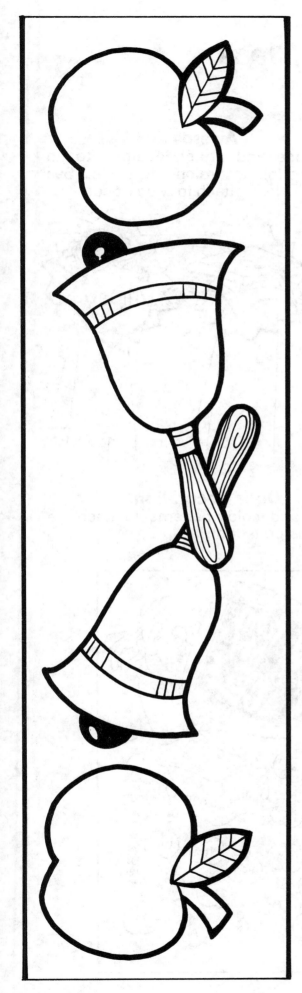

Copyright © 1990, Good Apple, Inc.

9

GA1141

Welcome to My Class
Crafts

Back to School
Table Decorations

Reproduce and color two of each pattern you wish to use. Cut a strip of paper 1" x 8". Form a loop and tape ends. Glue tab to the centers of matching illustrations.

Awards

Reproduce and attach designs to an aluminum foil accordion-fold circle. (See diagram.) Next, attach to wide ribbon.

Door Decoration

Enlarge and color patterns to decorate your classroom door.

Variations:

Reproduce patterns to desired size, color and glue to upside-down paper cup.

Glue designs to cans and small boxes covered with construction paper to make pencil holders and desk organizers.

Copyright © 1990, Good Apple, Inc.

GA1141

Count on Birthdays

Materials:

colored construction paper
white paper
markers
scissors
yarn

This bulletin board offers a personalized birthday greeting and teaches students to recognize the numerals 1 through 10 and their spellings. To make this board, enlarge and reproduce as many patterns as needed to desired size onto white paper. Color and laminate all pieces except the cake and bear birthday greeting. Give the birthday greeting to the student or students honored that day as a take-me-home.

Copyright © 1990, Good Apple, Inc.

11

GA1141

HAPPY BIRTHDAY

Copyright © 1990, Good Apple, Inc.

12

GA1141

Copyright © 1990, Good Apple, Inc.

GA1141

Copyright © 1990, Good Apple, Inc.

14

GA1141

Copyright © 1990, Good Apple, Inc.

Copyright © 1990, Good Apple, Inc.

16

GA1141

5 five 8

four 6 eight

4 six 9

three 7 nine

3 seven ten 0

Copyright © 1990, Good Apple, Inc.

17

GA1141

Count on Birthdays
Crafts

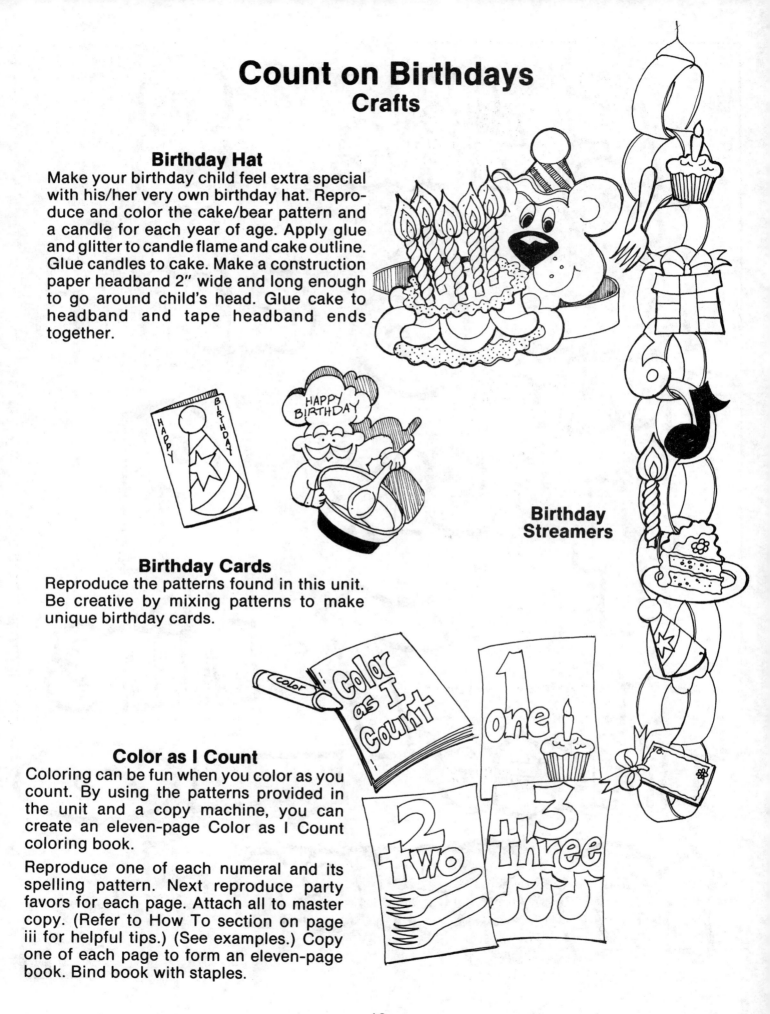

Birthday Hat

Make your birthday child feel extra special with his/her very own birthday hat. Reproduce and color the cake/bear pattern and a candle for each year of age. Apply glue and glitter to candle flame and cake outline. Glue candles to cake. Make a construction paper headband 2″ wide and long enough to go around child's head. Glue cake to headband and tape headband ends together.

Birthday Cards

Reproduce the patterns found in this unit. Be creative by mixing patterns to make unique birthday cards.

Birthday Streamers

Color as I Count

Coloring can be fun when you color as you count. By using the patterns provided in the unit and a copy machine, you can create an eleven-page Color as I Count coloring book.

Reproduce one of each numeral and its spelling pattern. Next reproduce party favors for each page. Attach all to master copy. (Refer to How To section on page iii for helpful tips.) (See examples.) Copy one of each page to form an eleven-page book. Bind book with staples.

Copyright © 1990, Good Apple, Inc.

18

GA1141

Signs of ~~Fall~~ Good Work

Materials:

scissors

paint or markers

Use this bulletin board to display fall art or good papers. For older students the board may be used to display current events or school activities. To begin cover the board with yellow paper. Reproduce and color enough leaf border to cover the bottom and two sides of board. Enlarge the children to desired size for the top of your bulletin board, filling in the remaining space with more reproducible leaf patterns. Enlarge tree pattern onto yellow background and color with paint or bright-colored markers. Hang students' work or current events from tree branches.

Copyright © 1990, Good Apple, Inc.

19

GA1141

Copyright © 1990, Good Apple, Inc.

20

GA1141

Good
Sights
of
Fall

Copyright © 1990, Good Apple, Inc.

21

Work

↑ _____ Place this line
on fold.

Copyright © 1990, Good Apple, Inc.

22

GA1141

Copyright © 1990, Good Apple, Inc.

23

GA1141

Signs of ~~Fall~~ Good Work
Crafts

Fall Wreath
Reproduce one tree pattern on copy machine for each child. Let each child color the picture. Glue the picture to a large paper plate. Using a paper punch, punch a hole on top center edge of the plate. Glue leaves and nuts you and your class have collected around the edge of the paper plate. Be sure not to cover the punched hole. Thread a piece of yarn through hole to hang. If leaves are not available in your area, you may make your own from construction paper, using leaves in pattern section as a guide.

Frames
Use child pattern and reproducible border pattern to frame good work or outstanding art.

Door Decoration
Enlarge title to fit your classroom door. Frame the rest of your door with reproducible leaf patterns. Use the award pattern from the Harvesttime unit. Reproduce one for each child in your class and write his/her name on the acorn. Tape the acorns to your class door.

Copyright © 1990, Good Apple, Inc.

GA1141

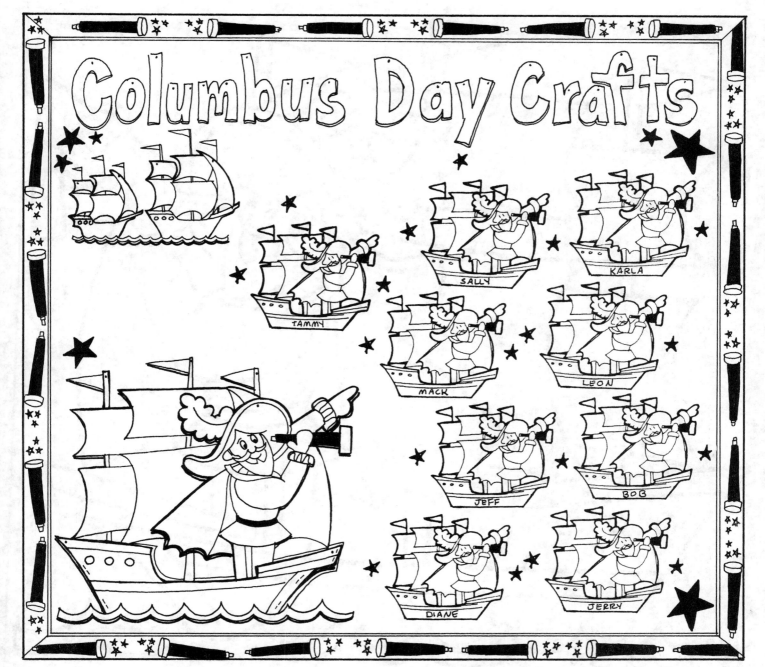

Columbus Day Crafts

Materials:

white mural paper	paint	scissors	glue
markers	tape	ribbon	

Use this holiday bulletin board to display your class crafts. See Columbus Crafty Craft activity on craft page. Begin your board by covering with white mural paper. Next reproduce and color enough border designs to go around the edge using colored markers. Enlarge ship to desired size onto mural paper, using the illustration above as a guide for positioning. Now reproduce the lower half of the large ship pattern onto brown paper. Add detail with black marker. Tape or staple the piece to the large ship on the board, leaving the top open. Reproduce and color one Columbus and several star patterns. Place Columbus into large ship and attach stars to board.

Paint blue waves on bulletin board as illustrated. Add flags cut from ribbon scraps to top of ships.

Copyright © 1990, Good Apple, Inc.

25

GA1141

Copyright © 1990, Good Apple, Inc.

26

GA1141

Columbus Day Crafts

Copyright © 1990, Good Apple, Inc.

27

GA1141

Columbus Day
Crafts

Columbus Crafty Craft

Reproduce one large ship and ship bottom for each child. After coloring the ships, staple the extra bottom to ship as illustrated, leaving the top open. Finally cut a triangle flag from ribbon and glue to ship. If desired reproduce, color and place Columbus inside.

Captain's Hat

To make this hat, you will need a large sheet of construction paper or large brown paper bag. Cut a long oval shape from the paper. (See illustration.) Now cut a 7" circle from the center. Reproduce and color enough border pattern to go around the cut out center. Tape the ends of the border strip together and tape to center of hat. Lift the end of one side of the hat brim up and over the top of the hat and staple in place. To decorate, reproduce several stars. Brush the stars with glue and sprinkle with glitter. Glue stars to hat. Finally cut a large feather shape from construction paper and fringe with scissors. Glue feather to hat.

Telescope

Make your own telescope from a paper towel tube, Dixie cup, plastic wrap, construction paper and pattern provided. Tape a small piece of plastic wrap to one end of the tube. Next cover the tube with black construction paper, gluing it in place. Reproduce and color a piece of bulletin board border and tape around paper cup. Cut a hole the size of a 50¢ piece out of the bottom of the cup and glue the cup to the end of the tube with plastic wrap on it.

Columbus Day Mobile

Reproduce patterns provided on page 27 onto lightweight or construction paper and color. Cut a strip 12" long and 2" wide from light-blue poster board. Next trim one edge of the strip to represent waves. Staple the ends together and attach Columbus Day patterns with string. (See illustration.)

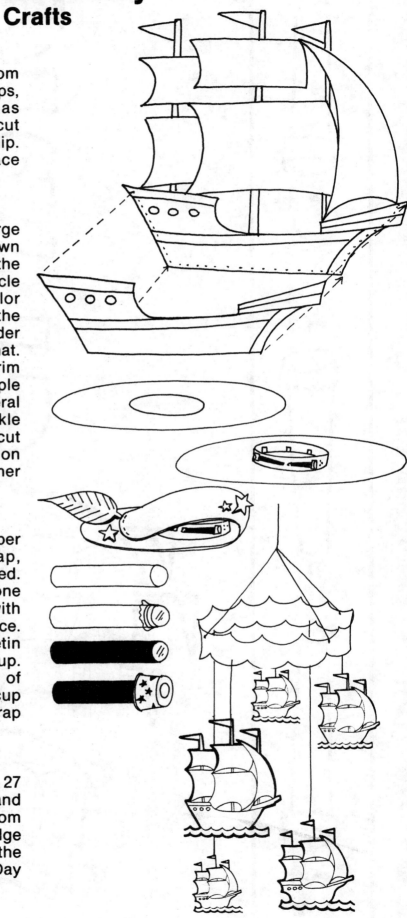

Copyright © 1990, Good Apple, Inc.

28

GA1141

Halloween Treats

Materials:

construction paper
scissors
white paper
markers or crayons

Display your spooky artwork or classroom papers on this Halloween bulletin board. To make this board, cover the board with orange paper. Next reproduce and color enough Halloween border pieces to cover entire bulletin board border. Enlarge the haunted house on brown paper, adding details with black markers. (The haunted house pattern is found on page 34.) Now enlarge title and reproduce enough slotted design patterns so each child can attach one to his/her work to be displayed.

Copyright © 1990, Good Apple, Inc.

GA1141

Copyright © 1990, Good Apple, Inc.

30

GA1141

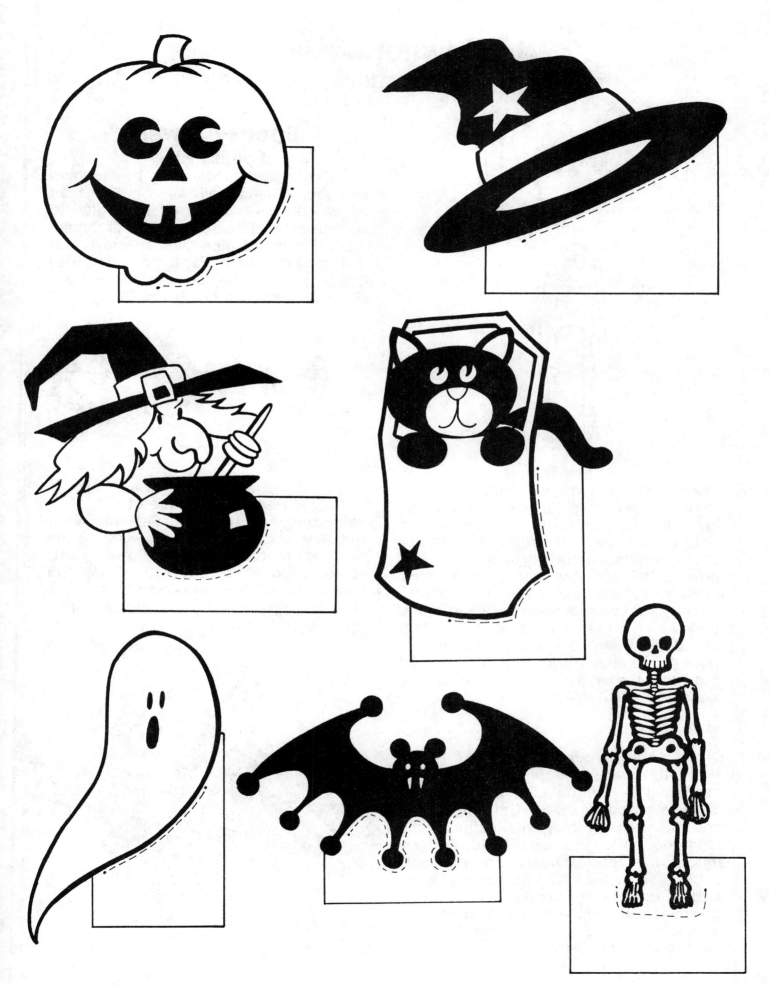

Copyright © 1990, Good Apple, Inc.

31

GA1141

Halloween Treats
Crafts

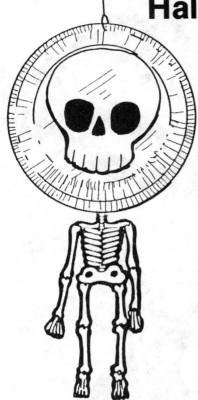

Shaky Bones

Spook your friends with your haunting shaky bones mobile. To make your mobile, enlarge and reproduce skeleton pattern onto white paper. Glue top of skeleton to bottom inside rim of one paper plate. Now draw a skeleton face using permanent marker onto that plate. (See illustration.) Finally, put one teaspoon of rice into one plate and glue other plate on top, sealing all edges. Punch small hole into top of plates and fasten with a string. Hang mobile outside in the wind or hold string with your hand and shake skeleton.

Halloween Headband

Make this easy and festive Halloween headband by reproducing and coloring patterns on pages 30-31. Cut out shapes and glue to a 2" strip of construction paper long enough to go around head. To turn this into a 3-D pop-up headband, glue small circle tabs to back of Halloween shapes and glue tabs to headband. Another creative tip is to glue bats and witches to strings. Glue the string to the back of headband. (See example.)

Spooky Jewelry
Spooky Ring

Make your own spooky ring by reducing and reproducing Halloween patterns on pages 30-31. Color the designs, glue to lightweight cardboard and cut out. Shape a small piece of pipe cleaner into a ring to fit child's finger. Tape the twist tie to the back of Halloween shape of your choice. (See illustration below.)

ring

bracelet

Haunting Bracelet

Wear this haunting bracelet with your Halloween costume this year. To make the bracelet, reproduce the Halloween patterns, color and cut out. Glue the characters to a strip of fabric or pipe cleaner long enough to fit around wrist. (See illustration.)

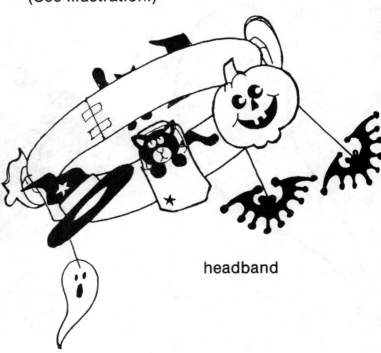

headband

Copyright © 1990, Good Apple, Inc.

GA1141

Where Are the Spooks?

Materials:

construction paper
markers
scissors

Where are the ghosts, bats and pumpkins? Use this Halloween bulletin board to teach special concepts in your classroom or just brighten your classroom in a spooky way. To create the board, first cover the background with grey construction paper. Enlarge the haunted house and tree onto brown paper, ghost and moon on white, pumpkins on orange, and bats on black paper. Bend the bat wings so they appear to fly and attach all pieces to the bulletin board. By moving the spooks around on the board, you are now ready to familiarize your students with above-below, top-bottom, outside-inside, left-right, first-middle-last, and near-far.

Copyright © 1990, Good Apple, Inc. GA1141

Copyright © 1990, Good Apple, Inc.

34

GA1141

Copyright © 1990, Good Apple, Inc.

35

GA1141

Where Are the Spooks?
Crafts

Dancing Pumpkins

Amaze your friends with a dancing pumpkin! To make the pumpkin, reproduce pumpkins onto orange paper. Lay a tissue flat and pick it up from the center. Tape the center of tissue to back of pumpkin so it forms a skirt. Finally, tape a piece of long thin thread to the top back of pumpkin's head. Now glue a second head to back of first head. Tip: Use smiling face on one side and frowning face on the other. To make your pumpkin dance, drop string with pumpkin over doorknob or chair. Stand away from the pumpkin, holding the string behind your back. By moving your hand up and down behind your back, you can make your pumpkin dance.

Walking Spooks

Help your students make their very own walking spooks! Reproduce walking spook pattern onto a sheet of typing paper (you can make four ghosts from one sheet of paper). Cut on solid line, and fold on the broken line. Let each child draw a spooky face on his/her ghost. Now tape a penny and string to each foot. (See illustration.) To make the ghost walk, place it on a smooth surface and gently pull one string at a time making one foot move in front of the other.

Spook Mobile

Make this holiday mobile by reproducing one haunted house and several ghosts, bats, and pumpkins onto construction paper. Draw detail with markers. Attach ghosts, bats, and pumpkins with string to haunted house. Finally fasten string to haunted house and hang it from ceiling.

Spook House Panorama

You can make your very own 3-D spook house to use as Halloween decoration or centerpiece. This house can be made with a quart milk carton or box of any size. Reproduce and color several ghosts, bats, and pumpkins. Glue or tape open end of box closed. Now cut off one large flat side of box or carton as illustrated. Glue or tape black, brown or orange construction paper around box. Using crayons draw windows, stairs, spiders, and other spooky things of your choice inside the box to look like haunted house. Glue yarn inside box to form cobwebs. Finally, cut small tabs of construction paper and glue them to the backs of ghosts and pumpkins. Bend tabs and glue and arrange little spooks in house. Bend bat wings and glue bats inside and outside house. Hang some bats from the ceiling with string.

Copyright © 1990, Good Apple, Inc.

GA1141

Harvesttime

Materials:

construction paper	markers
white paper	tape
scissors	staples
crayons	

Display your class harvest of good work on this seasonal bulletin board. Cover board with tan paper. Reproduce and color enough border designs to cover bulletin board border. Enlarge and color boy and girl with cornucopias and boy and girl with harvest baskets. Reproduce one acorn award for each paper to be displayed. Staple the acorn to corner of paper to display grade or good remarks.

Copyright © 1990, Good Apple, Inc.

GA1141

Harvestime

Copyright © 1990, Good Apple, Inc.

GA1141

Copyright © 1990, Good Apple, Inc.

39

GA1141

Copyright © 1990, Good Apple, Inc.

40

GA1141

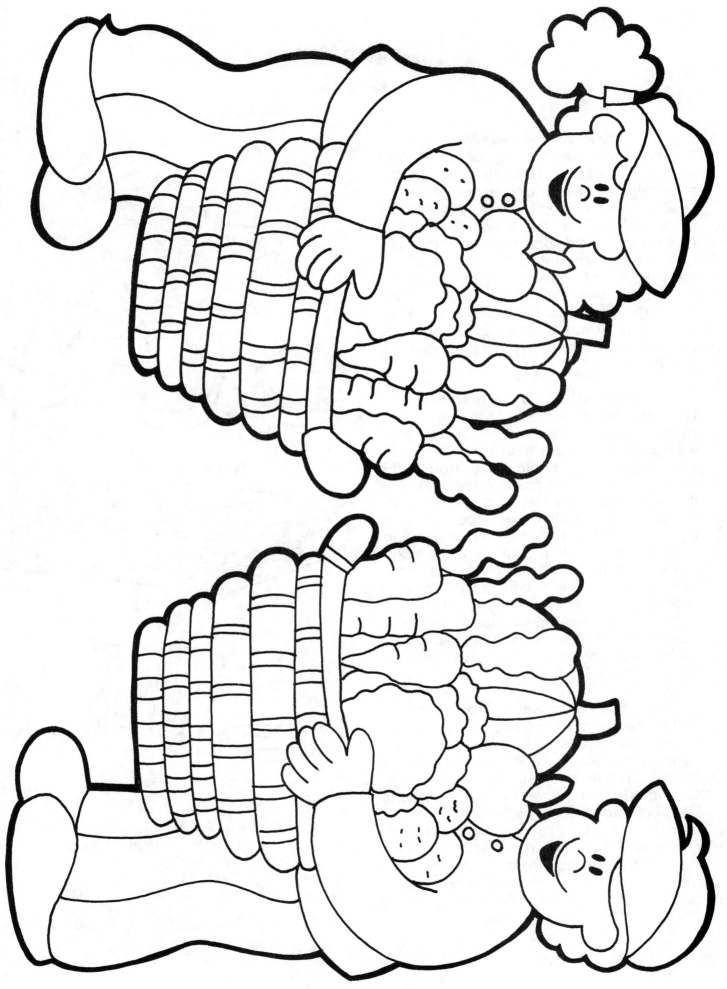

Copyright © 1990, Good Apple, Inc.

41

GA1141

Harvesttime
Crafts

Harvest Pendent

To make this harvest day pendent, give each child a small margarine tub lid and a variety of seeds, beans and leaves if available. Punch a small hole near the rim of each lid. Glue the seeds, beans and leaves to the inside bottom of lid using craft glue. When pendent is dry, string onto a long piece of yarn or ribbon. Finally, reproduce two acorn awards for each child. Punch two holes in each acorn as illustrated. String acorns on necklace and tie yarn ends. Now you have a harvest day pendent to give or keep.

Harvesttime Boat Races

Open up a walnut without breaking the half shell, and remove the nut meats. Lay your walnut open shell down on a piece of brown construction paper and trace around the shell. Cut out the traced shape and glue it to the shell. To make the sail cut a small triangle out of stiff white paper. Fold up the bottom of the triangle to form a flap. Glue the sail flap to nut shell as illustrated. Make a small lake from a 9" x 13" cake pan. Decorate the outside of the pan by reproducing and coloring enough border pattern to go around outside rim of pan. Line up the nut boats at one end of the water-filled pan and let the children blow them to the finish line.

Harvest Basket Hats

Cut a headband 2" wide and long enough to go around child's head out of brown construction paper. Tape the ends. Provide brown, orange and yellow 1" wide strips of construction paper for each student. Glue colored strips of paper onto hat band as illustrated. Provide a choice of reproduced patterns from pages 38-41 for the children to pick from. Color and glue the harvest pictures to the harvest basket hats. For added variety, glue fall leaves to the hats, if they are available.

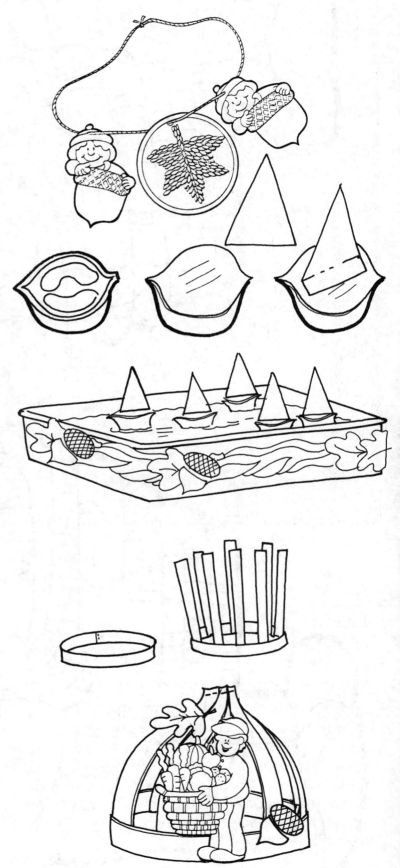

Copyright © 1990, Good Apple, Inc.

42

GA1141

We Are Thankful

Materials:

scissors
glue
orange construction paper

white paper
crayons
markers

Let your students show what they are thankful for during this holiday season. Cover the bulletin board with orange construction paper. Reproduce enough border designs to cover entire border. Turn your border into a 3-D border by reproducing and coloring several small turkey patterns and adding a small loop tab to the back. Glue the loop tab with turkey around bulletin board border as illustrated above. Using a copy machine, reproduce one large turkey for each student and let students illustrate and color what they are thankful for this holiday season in the center of the turkeys. Finally, enlarge and color remaining patterns and arrange on the bulletin board.

Copyright © 1990, Good Apple, Inc. GA1141

We Are Thankful

Copyright © 1990, Good Apple, Inc.

44

GA1141

Copyright © 1990, Good Apple, Inc.

45

GA1141

We Are Thankful
Crafts

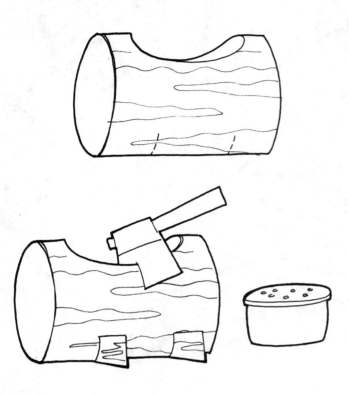

Thanksgiving Centerpiece

To make your Thanksgiving centerpiece, you will need a salt or oatmeal box with a lid. Cover box with brown construction paper. Cut a hole in the side of the box as illustrated. Make a base by cutting two strips of cardboard into 1" x 5" strips. Make slits in the bottom of the box and slip in the strips. This will keep your log from rolling around. With a black or brown marker, draw wood grain design on log and stand. Reproduce ax pattern onto lightweight cardboard and color. Make a slit in the top of the log and insert the ax. The centerpiece may be used to hold fresh flowers. Punch holes in the lid of a margarine tub, place the lid onto the tub and insert tub inside the log. Use the tub to hold fresh water and the holes in the top to hold flowers. The log is also great for holding dinner rolls or bread when lined with paper towels or to hold candy or holiday cookies.

Thanksgiving Place Mat and Coasters

Reproduce large turkey pattern onto heavy white drawing paper. Color turkey with paint, crayons or bright markers. Laminate picture with clear Con-Tact paper. To make the coasters, reproduce several small turkeys onto white paper. Color the turkeys and trim along edge. Laminate all the turkeys at one time leaving space around edge. Finally, using a large jar lid or round object larger than the turkey, trace around each coaster and trim on the line.

Turkey Napkin Rings

To make the napkin rings, reproduce and color as many small turkeys as needed. Using a paper punch, punch two holes in each turkey as illustrated. String orange yarn or ribbon through holes to tie around napkin. Another variation is to cut a strip of orange construction paper 1" x 5" and form a loop, gluing the ends together. Glue the turkey to the loop.

Use your centerpiece, place mats, coasters and napkin rings for your own classroom party or take-me-homes.

Copyright © 1990, Good Apple, Inc.

46

GA1141

Happy Thanksgiving

Materials:

scissors
construction paper
white mural paper
paint or bright markers

To make this bulletin board, cover the background with light-green paper. Next reproduce enough hat and pumpkin border to cover edge of bulletin board and color. Enlarge and color Pilgrims and Indians at the dinner table onto mural paper. Cut and place on the center of the board. Next reproduce and color the remaining patterns. Using old magazines or food store newspaper flyers, let the children cut out pictures of food for their Thanksgiving feast. Attach the pictures to the table on the bulletin board. This board can be used to teach the four basic food groups.

Copyright © 1990, Good Apple, Inc.

GA1141

Copyright © 1990, Good Apple, Inc.

48

GA1141

Copyright © 1990, Good Apple, Inc.

Happy Thanksgiving
Crafts

Pilgrim and Indian Puppets

Reproduce and color Pilgrim head. Glue the head to a small paper cup and let it dry. Punch a hole in the nose of the head large enough for a child's small finger to fit through. Glue the rim of the paper cup. Place the cup rim side down onto the center of an 8" x 8" piece of black crepe paper or fabric. When the glue is dry, cut a hole in crepe paper or fabric under the paper cup so child can insert finger through the puppet nose. Follow the same directions when making the Indian puppet except use brown crepe paper or fabric instead of black.

Turkey Puppet

Create your own simple turkey puppet by reproducing and coloring the turkey pattern provided onto heavy paper. Punch two holes for fingers in the lower half of the turkey.

Thanksgiving Stages

Here are two simple stages you and your class can make for a Thanksgiving puppet show. Place a box upside down on top of a table. Cut out the back of the box and the stage opening in the front of the box. Reproduce and color border design and other patterns provided and glue to the front and sides of the box. The second stage can be placed on the floor or on a table. To make this stage you will need a large piece of cardboard. Fold the box so it has three sides. Decorate by reproducing patterns provided.

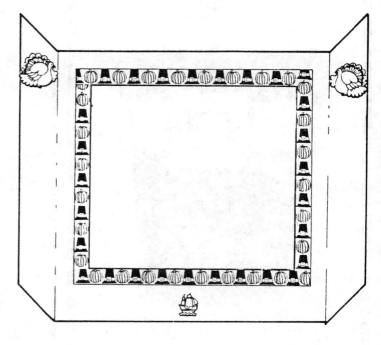

Copyright © 1990, Good Apple, Inc.

GA1141

Winter Wonderland

Materials:

construction paper
white mural paper
paint or markers

glue
cotton balls or Styrofoam peanuts

This seasonal bulletin board is also an activity to help children determine sizes—small, bigger, and biggest. Start making this board by covering the background with light-blue paper. Now enlarge title onto white mural paper and color with markers or paint. After positioning the title on the board, cut out enough 5″ circles with cotton balls or Styrofoam glued on them to cover the bulletin board border. Next reproduce the remaining patterns in three sizes each and attach to board in a winter scene arrangement.

Copyright © 1990, Good Apple, Inc.

51

GA1141

Copyright © 1990, Good Apple, Inc.

52

GA1141

Copyright © 1990, Good Apple, Inc.

53

GA1141

Winter Wonderland
Crafts and Activities

Winter Fun Necklace

Cut a piece of yarn long enough to go around your head and tie. Reproduce, color and cut out a variety of Winter Wonderland patterns for each child. Glue the characters to yarn and let dry.

Variation:

Use the directions above except use long strands of yarn and do not tie. When dry use as garland to hang around classroom and on doors as decoration.

Snowball Toss

Reproduce two copies of each pattern in this unit except the title. Arrange one of each pattern on a large spinner. Tape the other pattern to the floor. Have each child take a turn spinning the spinner and tossing a Styrofoam ball onto the appropriate pattern on the floor.

Snowman Puppet

To make this puppet you will need two matching snowmen, glue, cotton batting and a straw. Color the front of one snowman. Apply glue to the back of the snowman along the edge, except on the bottom. Place that snowman directly over matching snowman. When the glue is dry, lightly stuff snowman with batting, insert straw and glue opening shut. Write child's name on the front of the snowman.

Copyright © 1990, Good Apple, Inc.

GA1141

Oh, Christmas Tree

Materials:

scissors
glue
mural paper
construction paper

markers or crayons
sequins
scraps of lace

Use this bulletin board to assign classroom duties. Cover the board with white mural paper. Reproduce enough border to cover the edge of the board. Enlarge the tree pattern onto green construction paper and position on board. Trim with metallic garland. Reproduce all the ornament patterns onto colored paper. Give each child one ornament with his/her name on it. Decorate the ornaments with bright-colored markers or crayons. Glue on sequins and scraps of lace. Write a classroom duty on each branch of the tree. Hang the ornament that belongs to the student assigned that duty on that branch.

Copyright © 1990, Good Apple, Inc.

GA1141

Copyright © 1990, Good Apple, Inc.

56

GA1141

Copyright © 1990, Good Apple, Inc.

57

GA1141

Copyright © 1990, Good Apple, Inc.

GA1141

Copyright © 1990, Good Apple, Inc.

59

GA1141

Copyright © 1990, Good Apple, Inc.

60

GA1141

Copyright © 1990, Good Apple, Inc.

61

GA1141

Oh, Christmas Tree
Crafts

Christmas Tree Banner

Make this banner to hang on your class door or hallway. Enlarge tree pattern onto large sheets of construction paper, green mural paper or felt. Glue the top of the banner around a wooden dowel. Tie a thick piece of yarn 6" longer than the length of the dowel rod to the ends of the rod. Reproduce ornament patterns onto felt or colored paper and decorate with markers, lace and sequins. Glue ornaments on the tree. Trim the rest of the tree by gluing metallic garland, beads and sequins between the ornaments.

Christmas Stocking

Enlarge the stocking ornament onto two pieces of felt or construction paper. Glue around all edges except the top. Decorate the stocking with scraps of lace, yarn, glitter, crayons and markers. Punch a hole in top of the stocking and thread with yarn to hang.

Candy and Nut Holder Ornament

To make this ornament you will need one paper doily for each child. Fold the doily in half and then in half again. Form it into a cone shape and glue or tape where it joins. Staple a piece of ribbon on each side to make a handle. Reproduce an ornament pattern for each child. Color the picture and glue it to the side of the doily. Fill the holder with Christmas candy and nuts.

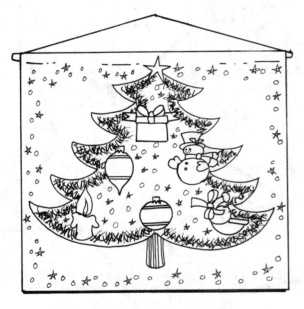

Easy Take-Me-Home Decorations

Reproduce and color ornament patterns. Decorate with shiny trims and lace scraps. Thread string through top for hanging.

Copyright © 1990, Good Apple, Inc.

GA1141

Countdown for Christmas

December

Countdown for Christmas

Materials:

white mural paper
red and green construction paper

scissors
markers

This bulletin board calendar will help you and your class count down the days till Christmas. Cover the board with white mural paper. Reproduce candy cane designs to go at the top of the board. Enlarge the title for the top of the board and color. Cut thirteen sheets of red and green construction paper in half. Draw a rectangle window on twenty-five halves, and cut on three sides to form a window that opens. Position the windows on the bulletin board to look like a calendar for December. Reproduce one pattern for each day of the month and attach to the board behind the appropriate window. Attach metallic garland to the inside edge of the bulletin board border.

Copyright © 1990, Good Apple, Inc.

GA1141

Copyright © 1990, Good Apple, Inc.

GA1141

Copyright © 1990, Good Apple, Inc.

65

GA1141

Copyright © 1990, Good Apple, Inc.

66

GA1141

Copyright © 1990, Good Apple, Inc.

67

GA1141

Countdown for Christmas
Crafts and Activities

Greeting Cards
Make greeting cards to deliver to family and special friends. Reproduce a variety of patterns. Color the patterns, cut out and glue to the front of a folded sheet of construction paper. Write a special message inside.

Countdown Mobile
Cut a large yellow star from poster board. Reproduce and color calendar patterns and hang from stars throughout the classroom. Let the children find the design that matches the day on the bulletin board calendar.

Holiday Wreath
On a thin piece of cardboard, draw a wreath 10" in diameter with a 6" center. Cut along the lines you have drawn. This is the base of your wreath. Cut ten 4" squares of green paper for each wreath. With scissors fray the edges of the green squares and glue on wreath. Reproduce and color a variety of patterns. Color and cut out the designs and glue several to each wreath. Make a bow from Christmas ribbon and glue to wreath. Finally, using a paper punch, punch a hole in center top and string a piece of yarn through to hang.

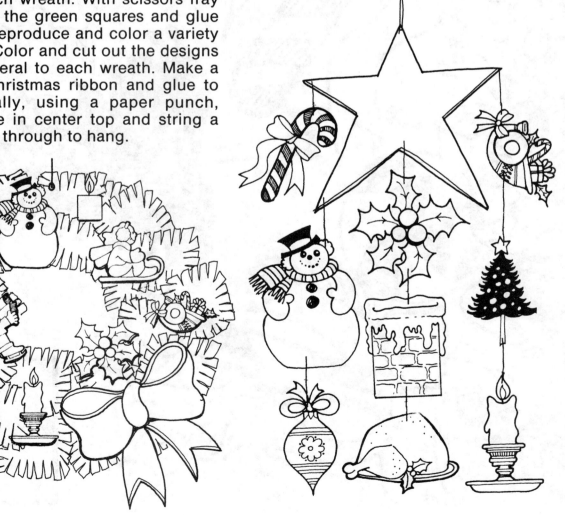

Copyright © 1990, Good Apple, Inc.

GA1141

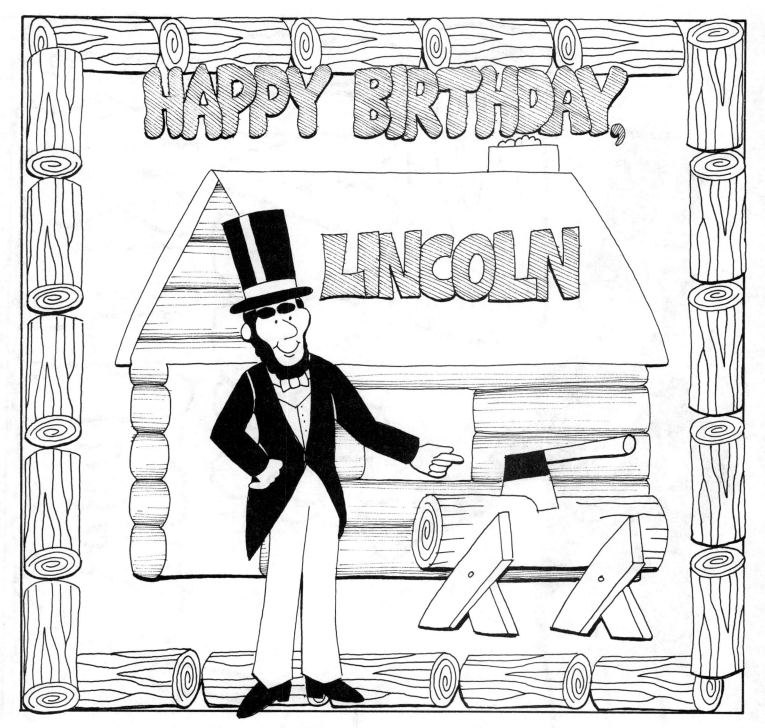

Happy Birthday, Lincoln

Materials:

construction paper
mural paper
markers or poster paints
scissors

To make this holiday bulletin board, first cover the background with pink paper. Next enlarge all patterns onto white mural paper and color or paint, adding details with markers. Cut out and attach all pieces to pink background. Reproduce and color enough log border pattern to cover the bulletin board border. Trim and tape logs to border.

Copyright © 1990, Good Apple, Inc.

GA1141

Copyright © 1990, Good Apple, Inc.

70

GA1141

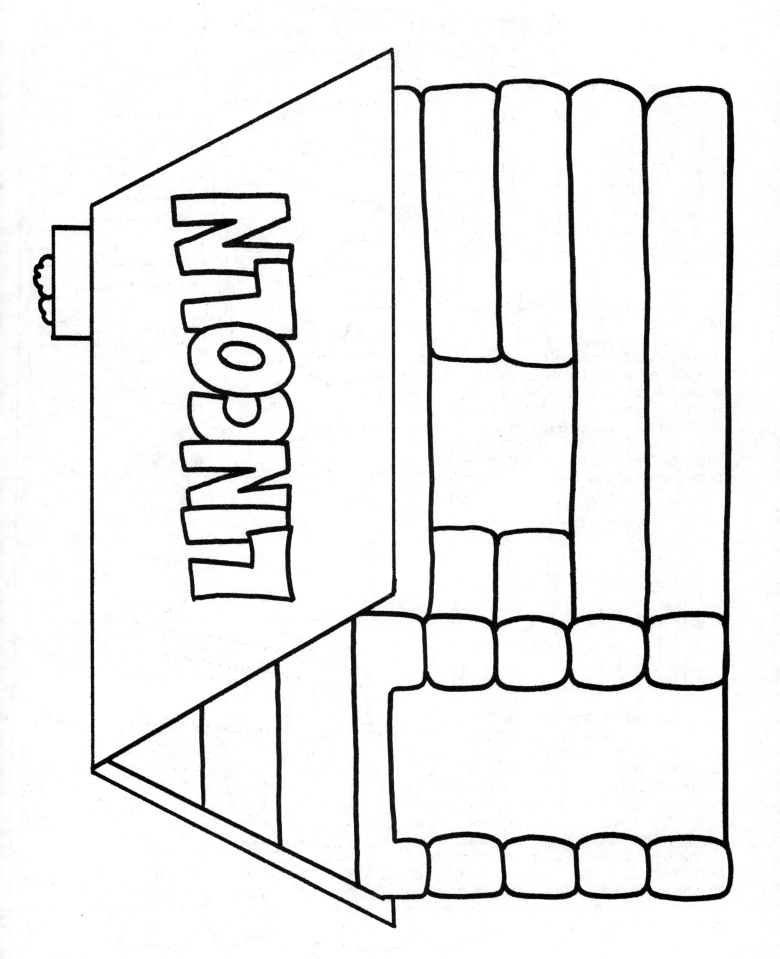

Copyright © 1990, Good Apple, Inc.

71

GA1141

Happy Birthday, Lincoln
Crafts and Activities

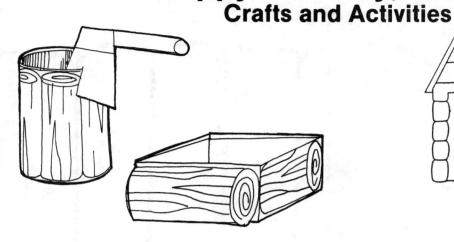

Lincoln Log Holders

Make these holiday decorations to hold your crayons, pencils and scissors, or use as take-me-home storage containers for the whole family. To start, collect a variety of cans and boxes. Reproduce log patterns from this unit to the desired sizes onto white drawing paper and colored construction paper. Color the pattern and glue to the containers, using the illustrations provided as examples.

Lincoln Logs for Math and Spelling Activities

To prepare for this activity, reproduce four cabin patterns. Color and glue the cabins to the sides of a box to be used as a storage box for your game pieces or flash cards. Reproduce several border logs onto brown construction paper. Use your Lincoln logs to sharpen counting, addition and subtraction skills. Turn the logs into flash cards to sharpen math, alphabet and spelling skills by writing problems, letters or words on the backs of the cards.

Mobile

Reproduce patterns from this unit onto lightweight cardboard or construction paper. Hang the figures from the log cabin. Attach a string to the top of the cabin for hanging.

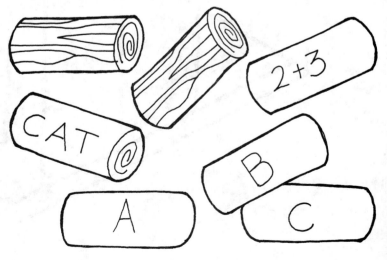

Copyright © 1990, Good Apple, Inc.

GA1141

Where Is It, Washington?

Materials:

construction paper
scissors
markers

This activity board not only brings up the question of who chopped down the cherry tree but where is it? Use this bulletin board to teach special concepts. Teach above-below, top-bottom, outside-inside, left-right, first-middle-last, near-far by repositioning the objects on the board. To make the board, cover the background with light-blue construction paper. Next enlarge and reproduce the patterns onto colored construction paper. Add details using markers. Reproduce and color enough cherry and flag border on copy machine to cover entire bulletin board border.

Copyright ©1990, Good Apple, Inc.   GA1141

Copyright © 1990, Good Apple, Inc.

74

GA1141

Copyright © 1990, Good Apple, Inc.

75

GA1141

Where Is It, Washington?
Crafts

Cheerful Cherry Necklace
Using cherry pattern and construction paper, make five cherries. Punch hole on top center of each cherry, string on yarn and tie.

Washington Mobile
To make this mobile, form a large cone shape from green construction paper. Next cut out red cherries using pattern as a guide, and glue them onto outside of cone. Reproduce and color Washington, dog, ax and extra cherries using patterns as a guide. Using different lengths of string, tie characters to lower edge of green cone. To complete your mobile, attach long string to top point of cone and hang it from the ceiling.

Washington Wreath
Help children create holiday 3-D take-me-home wreaths to hang on walls or doors. Reproduce and color one Washington, dog, ax and several cherries. Cut tabs ½" x 2" and glue ends together. Glue one round tab to back of each cherry. Next glue all pieces to a light-blue 12" circle of construction paper with an 8" cut out center. Fasten ribbon loop and bow to top to complete your 3-D wreath.

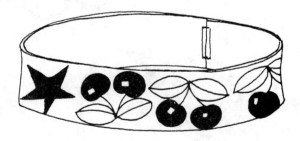

Washington Headband
Make this quick and easy headband by reproducing several cherry-flag border patterns. Color and trim the band pieces, taping them end to end until it is long enough to go around child's head. Tape ends to fit head.

Copyright © 1990, Good Apple, Inc.

76

GA1141

Valentine Countdown

Materials:

construction paper
scissors
markers, crayons or paint

Encourage your students to become familiar with the numbers 1 through 10 with the help of ten cute critters on a lively Valentine bulletin board. Begin this board by reproducing enough heart border to cover the bulletin board border. Next reproduce and color the numeral critters and numeral names. To complete this bulletin board, cut out enough pink and red hearts to represent each number, and display them on the board next to the appropriate number.

Copyright © 1990, Good Apple, Inc.

GA1141

9 nine 8 eight 6 four six seven 4

Copyright © 1990, Good Apple, Inc.

GA1141

7 1 2 +

5 3 teens

10 one

fivetwo

Copyright © 1990, Good Apple, Inc.

GA1141

three

Copyright © 1990, Good Apple, Inc.

GA1141

Copyright © 1990, Good Apple, Inc.

81

GA1141

Copyright © 1990, Good Apple, Inc.

82

GA1141

Copyright © 1990, Good Apple, Inc.

83

GA1141

Valentine Countdown
Crafts and Activities

Countdown Spinner Game

Familiarize students with numbers 1 through 10 and their spellings with this easy-to-make spinner. Reproduce one of each character and ten hearts onto construction paper. Cut a circle of lightweight poster board large enough to fit all critters on in a circle. Glue critters in position using illustration as a guide. Using bright marker, divide circle into pie shapes so each character is in a section. Write number and its spelling under each critter. Cut one arrow shape from black construction paper and connect to center of circle with a brad. Let each child take a turn spinning the spinner and counting out the appropriate number of hearts to match the numeral.

Variation:

Use the spinner for an addition or subtraction activity. As the child's skill level increases, increase the numbers on the spinner.

Valentine Headband

Reproduce one critter and enough hearts to spell out each child's name. Glue the critter and hearts to a construction paper headband 2″ wide and long enough to go around child's head. Glue or staple ends. Write the child's name on the hearts with markers, writing one letter on each heart.

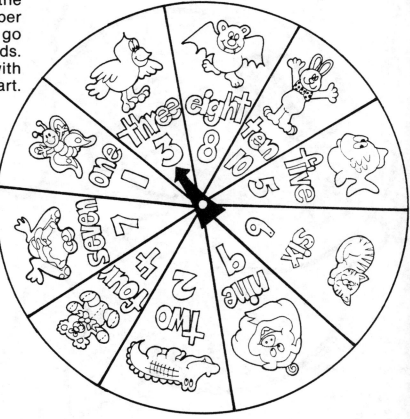

Copyright © 1990, Good Apple, Inc.

84

GA1141

Here Is My Valentine

Materials:

small cereal or cake mix boxes	ribbon
scissors	white paper
glue	paper doilies
lace scraps	sequins
construction paper	glitter

To make this bulletin board, reproduce and color enough reproducible border designs to go around board. Enlarge mailpersons and title to desired sizes. Let the children personalize their own cereal and cake mix boxes with scraps and materials provided. Leave space on each box for student's name. Add name using red or black markers.

Copyright © 1990, Good Apple, Inc.

GA1141

Copyright © 1990, Good Apple, Inc.

86

GA1141

Here Is My Valentine

Copyright © 1990, Good Apple, Inc.

87

GA1141

Here Is My Valentine
Crafts

Valentine Hat

To make this festive hat, mark off 4" from the base of a gallon milk jug or bleach bottle, and cut. Place it on the center of a 9" paper plate and trace around. Now cut out the center of the plate following traced line. Tape the top of hat in place. Decorate brim with reproducible border pattern and top of hat with hearts and lace. Wrap several strands of red yarn around brim of hat and tie in place, leaving long strands hanging down back. Tape pink and red hearts along strands. Glue a large heart to a pipe cleaner, and tuck the pipe cleaner between the crown and brim, taping in place.

Valentine Puzzle

Enlarge heart pattern onto lightweight cardboard. Reproduce a mailperson onto white paper for each child. Let him/her decorate both sides of heart and one side of the mailperson with crayons, markers or construction paper. When decorating with colored paper, be sure to cover entire back of paper with glue. Glue mailperson to heart. When heart is dry cut it into large pieces. Store puzzle in envelope.

Valentine Cards

Using large heart pattern, lay heart on the fold of a piece of construction paper. Trace and cut out the paper card. Let the child decorate the front of card using colored paper, sequins, glitter, fabric scraps and lace. Print *My Valentine* on the front. Cut out heart from aluminum foil using the same heart pattern. Glue the foil heart to the inside right side of the card.

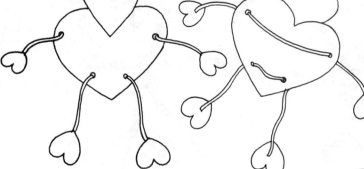

Dancing Valentine

This valentine on a stick can be a valentine dancer. Using patterns trace one large and one small heart onto lightweight cardboard and glue. (See illustrations.) Cut out tiny paper hands and feet. Punch four holes in large heart and thread two pieces of yarn through them. Glue paper hands and feet onto yarn ends. Using fringed paper and colored scraps, add hair and clothing. Tape your dancer to a pencil or Popsicle stick.

Copyright © 1990, Good Apple, Inc.

GA1141

Rainbow Race

Materials:

construction paper
white mural paper
markers
paint
scissors

As each child learns a color, a shamrock with his/her name is placed on that color on the rainbow. To make this bulletin board, cover the background with white mural paper. Next enlarge, color and cut out the leprechauns and pots of gold. Transfer the shamrocks onto green construction paper and arrange all pieces on board as illustrated above. Using poster paints or markers, color the rainbow directly on the mural paper. Reproduce enough small shamrocks so each child has five with his/her name to add to the board as the colors are learned.

Copyright © 1990, Good Apple, Inc.

GA1141

Copyright © 1990, Good Apple, Inc.

90

GA1141

Copyright © 1990, Good Apple, Inc.

91

GA1141

Rainbow Race
Crafts and Activities

I Wish Book
Let each child create his/her own I Wish Book. Reproduce one leprechaun with pot of gold pattern the size of a sheet of typing paper for each child. Using paper punch and yarn or a stapler, bind several sheets of paper and one leprechaun cover together. After coloring the cover, let the child draw or cut out from old magazines pictures of his/her wishes.

Door Decoration
Welcome your class or class parents with this cheerful holiday door decoration. Enlarge the leprechaun kids and shamrock patterns to the desired size and color. Decorate the edges of the shamrocks with an outline of glue and green glitter. Trim the buckles, buttons and coins with glue and gold glitter.

3-D Rainbow Wreath
To make this wreath, cut a 10" circle with a 6" cut out center from lightweight white poster board. Color ring of circle until it is covered. Reproduce one boy or girl leprechaun pattern and several green shamrocks for each child. Color leprechaun and glue it to the bottom center of wreath. Finally add loop tabs to the back of each shamrock and glue around wreath. Tie a loop of string or ribbon to the top of the wreath as a hanger.

Copyright © 1990, Good Apple, Inc.

GA1141

I Wish . . .

Materials:

green construction paper
markers
white paper
glitter

glue
magazines
scissors

Let this sparkling I Wish . . . activity board brighten your room this St. Patrick's Day. Reproduce one green shamrock for each child. Next help each child write his/her name in glue on the shamrock and sprinkle with glitter. Let dry. Enlarge the leprechaun on white paper and color using markers. Arrange leprechaun and shamrocks as illustrated above on bulletin board. Now pass out old magazines or catalogs and let each child cut out a picture of something he/she wishes for.

After each child talks about his/her wish picture, attach a little green lucky shamrock to the corner and place on board.

Copyright © 1990, Good Apple, Inc.

GA1141

Copyright © 1990, Good Apple, Inc.

94

GA1141

Copyright © 1990, Good Apple, Inc.

95

GA1141

I Wish. . .
Crafts

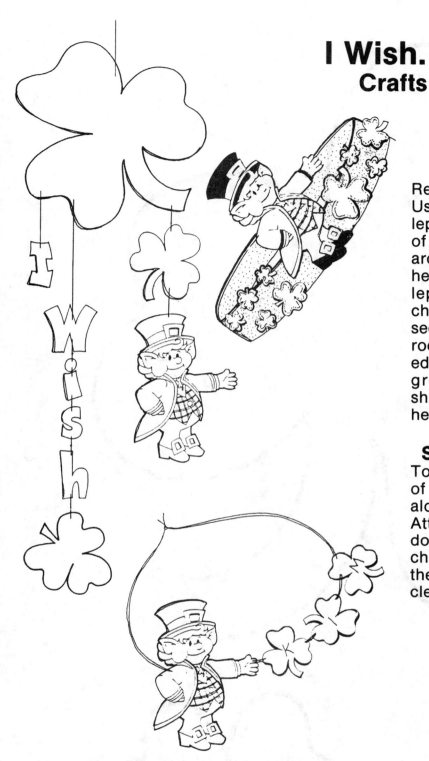

Lucky Leprechaun Hat
Reproduce and color one leprechaun. Using green and gold glitter, decorate the leprechaun. Cut a 3″ wide headband out of construction paper, long enough to go around child's head. Glue the center of the headband to the lower one third of the leprechaun. Fit the headband around child's head to measure and staple ends securely. Finally reproduce several shamrocks. Spread a thin line of glue along the edge of each shamrock and sprinkle with green and gold glitter. When the shamrocks are dry, glue them along the headband.

St. Patrick's Day Door Decoration
To make this door decoration, run strips of twisted crepe paper streamers vertically along door. Enlarge and color leprechaun. Attach the leprechaun to the center of the door. Reproduce one shamrock for each child and write his/her name on it. Fasten the shamrocks to the door streamers, using clear tape.

Personalized Lucky Necklace
Each student can have his very own personalized necklace by reproducing one leprechaun to the desired size and one shamrock for each letter of the student's name. Color the pattern pieces and write each letter of the child's name on a separate shamrock. Using a paper punch, make a hole in each piece and string letters onto yarn or ribbon in the proper order. Secure ends with a knot.

Copyright © 1990, Good Apple, Inc.

GA1141

Easter Egg Hunt

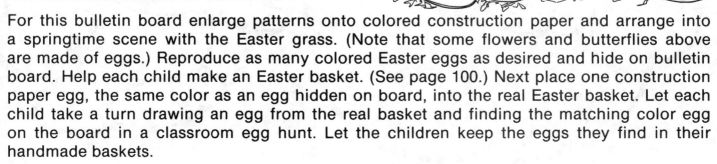

Materials:

construction paper
scissors
Easter grass
real Easter basket
one handmade basket for each child

For this bulletin board enlarge patterns onto colored construction paper and arrange into a springtime scene with the Easter grass. (Note that some flowers and butterflies above are made of eggs.) Reproduce as many colored Easter eggs as desired and hide on bulletin board. Help each child make an Easter basket. (See page 100.) Next place one construction paper egg, the same color as an egg hidden on board, into the real Easter basket. Let each child take a turn drawing an egg from the real basket and finding the matching color egg on the board in a classroom egg hunt. Let the children keep the eggs they find in their handmade baskets.

Copyright © 1990, Good Apple, Inc.

GA1141

Easter Egg Hunt

Copyright © 1990, Good Apple, Inc.

98

GA1141

Copyright © 1990, Good Apple, Inc.

GA1141

Easter Egg Hunt
Crafts

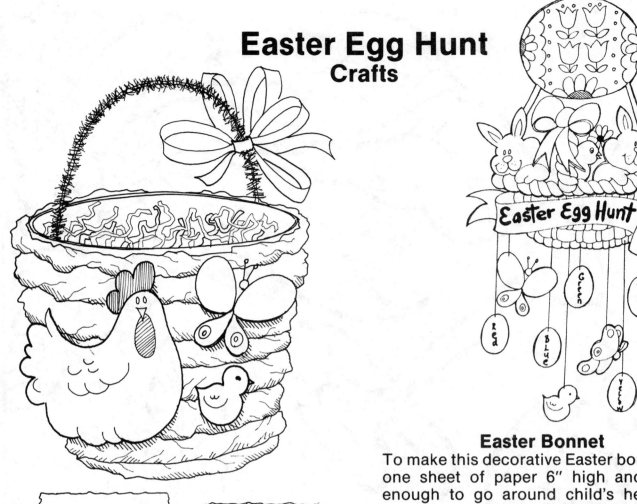

Easter Basket

To make the Easter basket, begin by gluing each end of one pipe cleaner to the outside edge of a plastic flowerpot, using craft glue. Next crunch strips of crepe paper streamers as illustrated. Glue the strips of crunched paper around outside edge of the flowerpot. When the glue is dry, give each child an assortment of animals, flowers and butterflies reproduced from the pattern pages to color. Glue the colored designs to the basket. Finally, tie a ribbon bow on the pipe cleaner handle and fill with Easter grass.

Easter Bonnet

To make this decorative Easter bonnet, cut one sheet of paper 6″ high and long—enough to go around child's head. Cut seven tabs 1″ deep as shown in illustration. Wrap the band around child's head to fit and staple ends. Next bend tabs toward center. Apply glue to each tab. Place one paper plate upside down onto glued tabs and let dry. Reproduce, color and glue desired patterns to the bonnet. Staple two ties made from ribbon onto the hat brim. If desired, decorate the top of hat with additional ribbon and scraps of lace.

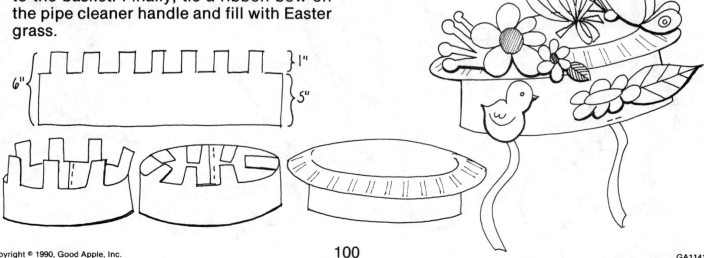

Copyright © 1990, Good Apple, Inc.

GA1141

Bunny Matchup

Materials:

construction paper
yarn
scissors
jelly beans
basket

To make this bulletin board, start by enlarging the title and position on board with the yarn as illustrated. Next enlarge one bunny and clothes. Attach large bunny to board. Reproduce one bunny pattern same size as pattern for each child. Put enough colored jelly beans in a basket so each child can have one. Then reproduce on colored paper enough sets of clothes the same colors as the jelly beans in the basket. Attach the little sets of clothes to the board. As a class project let all the students help the teacher dress the large bunny. Next let each child draw a jelly bean from the basket and find the set of clothes on the board that matches the color of the jelly bean. Glue the clothes on the bunnies and pin to the board for a colorful Easter display.

Copyright © 1990, Good Apple, Inc.

GA1141

Copyright © 1990, Good Apple, Inc.

102

GA1141

Copyright © 1990, Good Apple, Inc.

103

GA1141

Bunny Matchup
Crafts

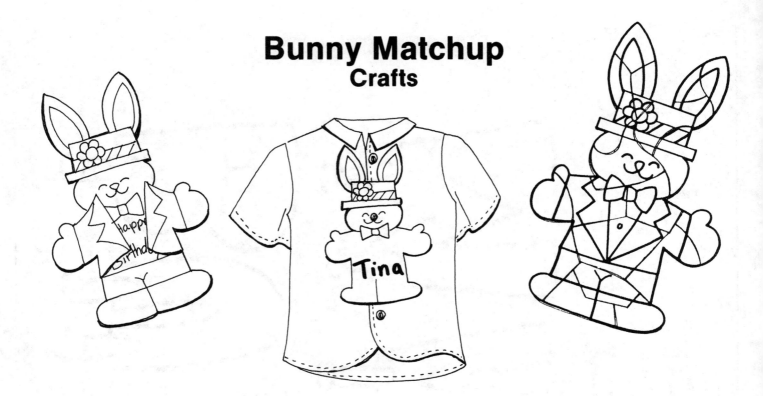

Bunny Easter Greeting

Use this card as an Easter greeting or everyday all-occasion card. Reproduce one bunny and set of clothes for each child. Color all clothes. Glue hat, tie and pants in position. Write your greeting on the bunny's stomach. Finally, cut the jacket in half as illustrated. Apply glue to back side of sleeves only and position jacket in place on the bunny.

Button Name Tag

Reproduce one bunny, hat and tie for each child. Glue hat and tie in place and write child's name on stomach. Using X-acto knife or sharp scissors, make ¼" slit across bunny nose. Button tag onto child's shirt or blouse. If there is not a button on the clothing, attach tag with a pin.

Bunny Puzzle

Enlarge bunny and clothing. Color clothing and glue into position. Make sure clothing is completely glued down. Let dry. Cut bunny into large shapes. Store your puzzle in a large envelope.

Door Decoration

Copyright © 1990, Good Apple, Inc.

104

GA1141

Hurray for May

Celebrate spring in your classroom with this Hurray for May bulletin board. This board can be a great discussion starter for signs and activities of the spring and summer months that lie ahead.

Materials:

construction paper
scissors

stick, string, fishing bobber
fishing pole (optional)

crayons
markers

Enlarge patterns to the desired size with an overhead projector and transfer them to construction paper. To make tree leaves, cover those areas on the bulletin board with large sheets of green paper. Next cut or tear clusters of leaf shapes and overlap them around the edge of the area. Grass is made from strips of green paper 4" high with cuts made 3" deep every ½". (See illustration above.)

Transform your bulletin board into a classroom activity by enlarging and reproducing on the copy machine enough butterflies, flowers, birds and worms so each child can cut and color his own to add to the board. For variation, help children decorate their critters using craft glue, paper scraps, sequins, glitter or yarn.

Copyright © 1990, Good Apple, Inc.

GA1141

Copyright © 1990, Good Apple, Inc.

106

GA1141

Copyright © 1990, Good Apple, Inc.

107

GA1141

Hurray for May
Crafts and Activities

Reproduce patterns and use them to reinforce counting skills.

Color or reproduce characters onto colored construction paper. Use them to help teach recognition of primary and secondary colors.

May Basket

For each basket you will need two identical hearts cut from two sheets of construction paper and one handle made of ½" wide ribbon or a strip of construction paper 1" wide and 12" long. Next staple handle to heart and trim heart with scraps of lace if available. (See illustration.) Reproduce several flowers and one bird and butterfly for each child to color or decorate with glitter and sequins. Glue bird to one side of basket and butterfly to the other. Fill basket with flowers for a fun May basket gift.

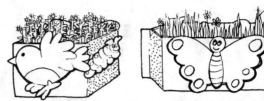

Windowsill Garden Trays

For this project you will need a clean, empty milk carton (any size), potting soil and flower seeds. (Choose flower seeds that take the least amount of time to germinate.) Cut off top section of milk carton or cut in half depending on size of container. (See illustration.) Reproduce birds, butterflies and worms. Let each child decorate four. Glue one critter to each side of carton. Help fill tray half full of soil. Plant seeds according to directions. Place tray in warm sunny spot and water as often as needed. Watch them grow!

May Mobile

May Headband

Fluttering Butterfly Pencil Decoration

First decorate butterfly. Using a paper punch, carefully punch a hole at each end of butterfly body. Bend wings up and insert pencil. Make butterfly flutter by rolling the pencil between hands. You can also make a flying bird and wiggle worm using the same basic instructions. (See illustration.)

Copyright © 1990, Good Apple, Inc.

GA1141

Happy Mother's Day

Materials:

construction paper
mural paper
markers or paint
scissors

Use this bulletin board to display art to be used as Mother's Day gifts. To make this board, reproduce and color enough crowns or hearts to cover entire bulletin board border. Attach to border. Next enlarge onto mural paper the title and Mom with flowers. Color them with markers or paint, adding details with markers. Reproduce one gift tag for each child to be fastened onto the gift for the mothers. Display the art with the gift tags on the bulletin board.

Copyright © 1990, Good Apple, Inc.

GA1141

Copyright © 1990, Good Apple, Inc.

110

GA1141

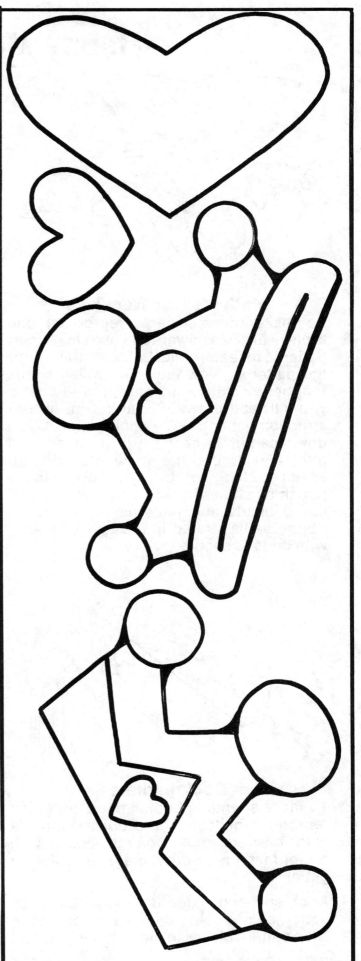

Copyright © 1990, Good Apple, Inc.

GA1141

Happy Mother's Day
Crafts

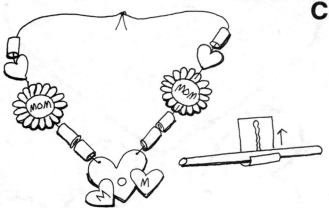

Mother's Day Necklace

To make this necklace, reproduce one triple heart, two flowers and two small heart patterns for each child. Let each child color the patterns. Now make six rolled beads for each necklace. To make rolled beads, you will need straws, glue and strips of construction paper 1" x 3". Apply a line of glue down center of each strip of paper. Roll the paper around the straw, glue-side up as illustrated. Let the glue dry. Finally punch two holes in each pattern piece and string beads and patterns onto yarn or ribbon as illustrated in example. Tie knot with ends to secure.

Sun Catcher

To make your Mother's Day sun catcher, reproduce two Mom with flower patterns on white paper for each child. Assist your students with cutting out the centers of random flowers, making sure to cut out the same flowers on each piece. Next apply glue to the back of one pattern and front of other. Slip a piece of colored tissue paper in between the two patterns, lining up the flower holes. When the glue is dry, punch a hole in top of sun catcher and add a string for hanging. Hang your sun catcher in a sunny window or from a ceiling light as a mobile.

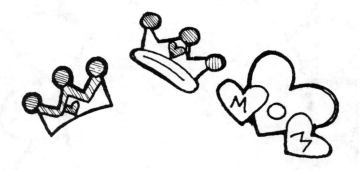

Bookmarkers

To make sparkling bookmarkers for Mom, reproduce bulletin board border and cut to the desired length. Color the design with bright markers and decorate with glue or glitter.

Another marker idea is to reproduce toy patterns onto colored construction paper. Glue pattern pieces to different lengths and widths of ribbon.

Refrigerator Magnets

For an easy-to-make Mother's Day take-me-home, reproduce desired patterns onto white paper. Color and decorate with glue and glitter. Glue the pattern to a piece of lightweight cardboard and trim. Finally, glue a small piece of magnetic tape to the back of your design and let dry.

Copyright © 1990, Good Apple, Inc.

GA1141

Moms and Babes

Materials:

large sheets of construction paper
scissors
crayons
markers

Let this bulletin board help you teach animal recognition and matchup in your classroom. To make this board, first cover board with colored paper. Next enlarge animal patterns onto white paper. Color.

Cut out and laminate the animals for durability now and in the future, or let the class participate in coloring. (This activity may be used on Mother's Day or any day!)

Copyright © 1990, Good Apple, Inc.

113

GA1141

Copyright © 1990, Good Apple, Inc.

114

GA1141

Copyright © 1990, Good Apple, Inc.

115

GA1141

Copyright © 1990, Good Apple, Inc.

116

GA1141

Copyright © 1990, Good Apple, Inc.

GA1141

Copyright © 1990, Good Apple, Inc.

118

GA1141

Copyright © 1990, Good Apple, Inc.

GA1141

Moms and Babes
Crafts

Pop-Up Animal Habitat

Reproduce one mom and matching babe for each child. Let each child color his/her animals. Next have children discuss, draw and color the animals' habitats on sheets of white paper. Finally cut a scrap of paper to form a loop and glue it to the back of each animal and attach to the appropriate drawing.

Variation:

Using the same concept as above, form a classroom mural.

Mobile

To make this mobile, reproduce one large heart. Write *Moms and Babes* on the heart with a bold marker. Reproduce and hang a mother and its baby on each string. Hang as many varieties of animals as desired onto each heart. Attach a string to the heart for hanging.

Take-Me-Home Necklace

Help each child make moms and babes matching necklaces. Paint different shapes and sizes of macaroni with tempera paint. Reproduce one matching mom and babe for each child to color. Punch a hole in each animal for stringing. String one animal and a variety of colored macaroni and pasta onto each string. Tie the ends securely.

Variation:

Glue each animal onto an appropriate size paper heart. Punch a small hole in the heart for stringing.

Copyright © 1990, Good Apple, Inc.

GA1141

Shape Up for Summer

Materials:

colored construction paper
scissors
markers
white mural paper

Use this scenic bulletin board to teach shape recognition, by matching cut out shapes to objects found in the picnic scene. This board can be made two ways. The first way is to enlarge the patterns provided onto construction paper and arrange into a colorful picnic scene as illustrated above. The second method is to enlarge with overhead projector and trace the above illustration onto a sheet of mural paper large enough to cover your bulletin board. Next using crayons or markers, let the class color the picnic scene.

Copyright © 1990, Good Apple, Inc. 121 GA1141

Copyright © 1990, Good Apple, Inc.

122

GA1141

Copyright © 1990, Good Apple, Inc.

123

GA1141

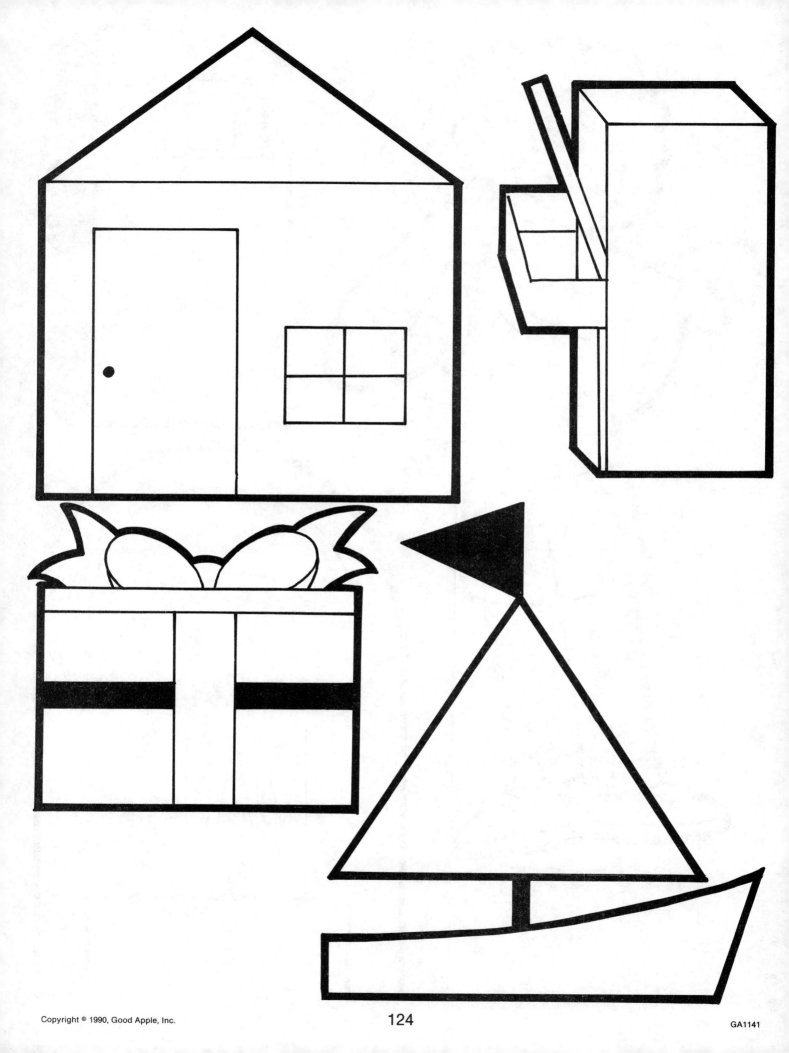

Copyright © 1990, Good Apple, Inc.

124

GA1141

Copyright © 1990, Good Apple, Inc.

125

GA1141

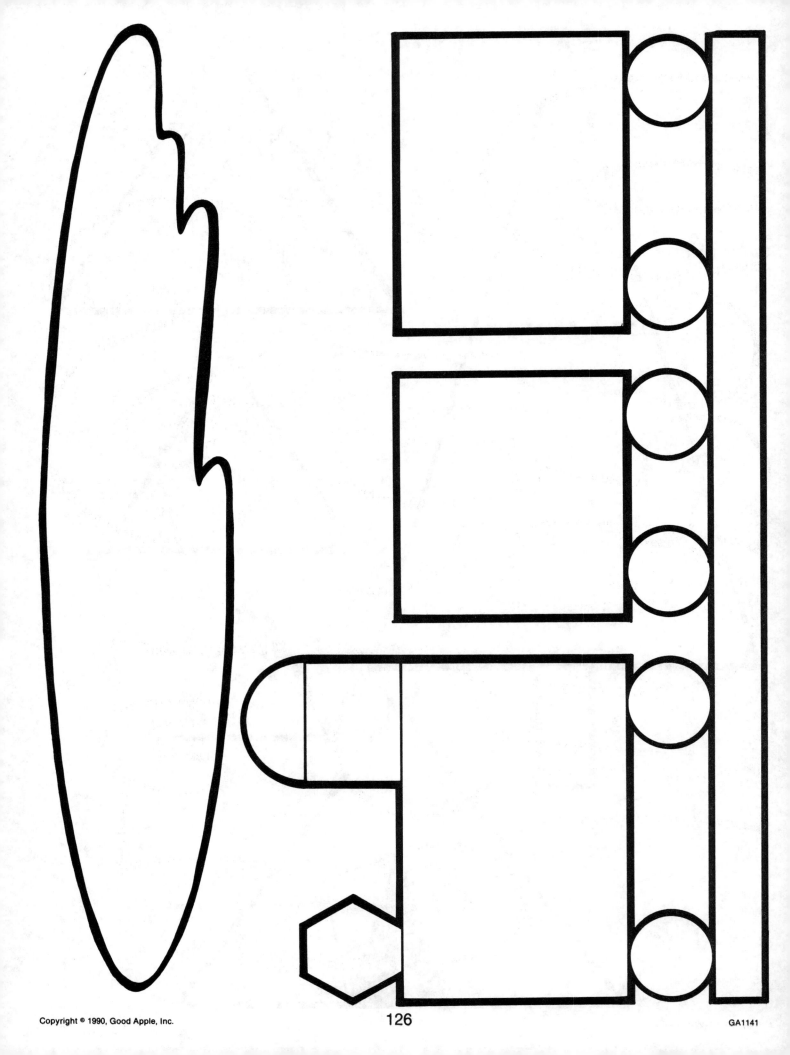

Copyright © 1990, Good Apple, Inc.

126

GA1141

Copyright © 1990, Good Apple, Inc.

GA1141

Shape Up for Summer
Crafts and Activities

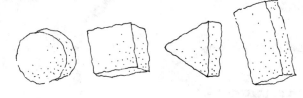

Shape Toss

This activity helps reinforce shape recognition and coordination. Prepare for this game by enlarging and reproducing all patterns except the title onto white paper and color. Tape the objects to the floor in a random manner. Next cut a 5″ circle, triangle, square and rectangle from a chunk of Styrofoam. Place the Styrofoam shapes in a basket. To play the game, have each child take turns standing behind a designated tape line, closing his eyes and drawing a shape from the basket. After a shape is drawn from basket, the child opens his/her eyes and tries to toss the shape on a floor pattern that contains the same shape.

Shape Mobile

Reproduce and color patterns from this unit and assemble as illustrated.

School Paper Tote

Let the children carry home their class projects with the least amount of damage in this easy-to-make tote. Cut two sheets of lightweight cardboard or poster board. Using packing tape or staples, lay the two pieces together and secure the bottom and two sides together. To make a tote handle, punch two holes 4″ apart on the top center of each side of the tote. Tie one 10″ piece of twine through each two holes on each side of the tote and secure ends with a knot. Decorate the tote by gluing reproduced and colored patterns on the sides of the tote. Finally personalize each tote by writing the child's name on the side.

Copyright © 1990, Good Apple, Inc.

GA1141

Happy Father's Day

Materials:

construction paper
mural paper
markers or paint
scissors

Use this bulletin board to display art to be used as Father's Day gifts. To make this board, reproduce enough yellow crowns to cover entire bulletin board border and attach to border. Next enlarge dad banner and boy and girl onto white mural paper. Color with paint or markers, adding details with markers. Reproduce one slotted gift tag for each child to be fastened onto the gifts for their fathers. Display the art with the gift tags on the bulletin board.

Copyright © 1990, Good Apple, Inc.

GA1141

Copyright © 1990, Good Apple, Inc.

GA1141

To:

To:

Copyright © 1990, Good Apple, Inc.

131

GA1141

Happy Father's Day
Crafts

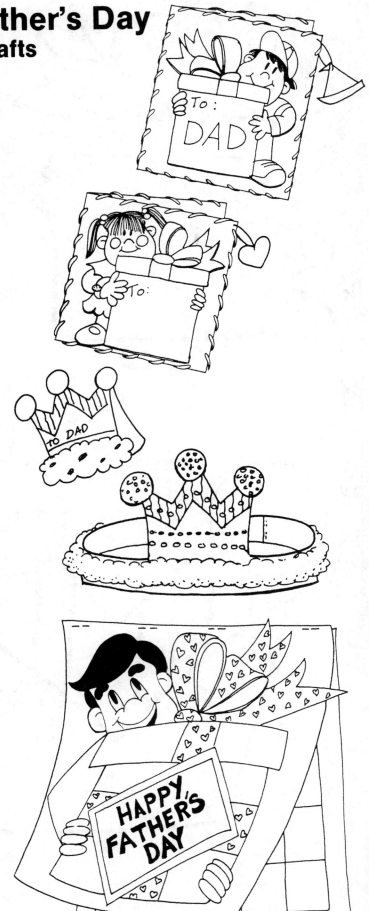

Father's Day Cards

Reproduce one boy or girl pattern for each child. Fold a sheet of construction paper in half and glue the child pattern onto the front. Color the cards and write a personal message inside. Punch holes around edge of front of card ½" to 1" apart. Let the children stitch bright-colored yarn in holes, starting at the upper right corner. When stitching is complete and before the ends of yarn are tied together, string a gift tag with child's name on it onto yarn and tie a bow.

Crown Card

Cut out two crowns for each child. Apply glue only to the balls on top of the crown. Press the crowns together. Glue cotton balls to the bottom rim of the front crown and let dry. Write a Father's Day message inside.

Father's Day Crown

Enlarge the crown pattern and glue to a construction paper headband 2" wide and 15" long. Glue cotton balls or batting along the bottom of the crown and along the headband. Now decorate the top of the crown with sequins and glitter. Let the crown dry and staple headband ends together.

Father's Day Calendar

Help the children make an easy Father's Day take-me-home. Enlarge the Father's Day banner big enough to cover a sheet of paper 8½" x 11". Using a thin black marker, trace each month from a current calendar (not larger than 8½" x 11") onto white typing paper. Reproduce the tracings on a copy machine so each student has a copy of each month. After the children color their banner calendar covers, attach the cover to the stack of calendar months by stapling through all along the top.

Copyright © 1990, Good Apple, Inc.

GA1141

Happy Birthday, U.S.A.

Let this cheerful bulletin board bring a Fourth of July celebration right into your classroom.

Materials:

construction paper	glitter	colored markers
mural paper	scissors	glue

Enlarge bears and cake to desired size and transfer to white mural paper. Color with bright markers. Keep in mind the holiday colors—red, white and blue. Enlarge and transfer candles and stars to construction paper. To make firecracker, roll a rectangular sheet of red construction paper (5" x 6") into cylinder and glue seam to hold shape. Cut star bursts from yellow construction paper and with the help of the children, decorate with dabs of glue and glitter. Glue star burst tabs to inside of firecrackers. Delightful sparklers are made by applying glue and glitter to one side of construction paper. Cut paper into thin strips stopping 2" from bottom. Roll paper, glitter side in, into tight roll and staple bottom. (See illustration.) Fluff sparkler strips outward from center.

Copyright © 1990, Good Apple, Inc.

133

GA1141

Copyright © 1990, Good Apple, Inc.

134

GA1141

Copyright © 1990, Good Apple, Inc.

135

Happy Birthday, U.S.A.
Crafts

Hat

Reproduce bear banner pattern. Color and decorate with glitter. Glue to a construction paper headband 2" wide and staple ends together. Let each child cut stars out of yellow construction paper and glue to headband.

Door Decoration

Use bulletin board patterns to create this door decoration. Instead of the round firecrackers, cut rectangles from 3" x 5" red paper. Attach tab and star burst to red rectangle. Write the children's names on the firecrackers.

Noisemaker

Cut a 1" x 6" strip of cardboard and staple to inside of a small paper plate. Lay a few pieces of macaroni inside the plate and staple another plate to the first one. Punch holes around the plate rim. Put a string through each hole, and then through several pieces of drinking straw cut into beads. A bell may also be added. Tie the ends of the string to secure. Reproduce the pattern of your choice from this unit. Color and glue the designs to the plates.

Firecracker Necklace

To make this necklace, reproduce one bear with flag for each child. Color the bear and flag and glue to lightweight cardboard if desired. Trim edges. Punch a hole in the top of the hat and string onto yarn or ribbon. To make firecracker beads, you will need several 5" pieces of yarn and 1" x 4" strips of red construction paper. Apply glue to one side of a strip of red paper. Lay a piece of yarn on one end of the glued paper. Fold the edge of the paper over the yarn and roll the rest of the paper around the yarn. Clip with a clothespin to hold until dry. When firecracker is dry, tie the yarn onto necklace. Trim the excess yarn. Dab a bit of glue onto the knot and sprinkle with gold glitter. To make a simpler variation of the firecracker bead, cut drinking straws into 1" pieces. Glue one end of the yarn to the inside of the straw bead. When it is dry, tie the other end of the yarn to the necklace. Trim the excess yarn. Dab a bit of glue onto the knot and sprinkle with glitter.

Copyright © 1990, Good Apple, Inc.

GA1141

Dream Vacations

Materials:

light-blue mural paper   markers   batting   old magazines
construction paper   crayons   scissors

Use this bulletin board as a discussion starter and a display of your students' dream vacations. Cover the board with light-blue mural paper. Enlarge patterns onto white and colored construction paper and color with bright markers. Attach boy and girl to background. Using white batting, form a large circle of clouds along inside of bulletin board border. Now attach plane, train, sunshines, car, ship and title. Finally, let your students add their artwork. Cut a sheet of white paper into the shape of a cloud. Have each child draw a picture of his/her dream vacation on the cloud and glue cotton balls or batting around the edge.

Variation:

Cut dream location or activity from magazine and glue on chart.

Copyright © 1990, Good Apple, Inc.

137

GA1141

Dream Vacations

Copyright © 1990, Good Apple, Inc.

138

Copyright © 1990, Good Apple, Inc.

139

GA1141

Dream Vacations
Crafts and Activities

Vacation Time Calendar

This easy-to-make calendar is a great vacation take-me-home for Mom and Dad. Cut out the vacation months from a calendar and redraw your own. Reproduce enough for each student.

Decide what size paper you will need to have room for the calendar and vacation pictures. Give each child a sheet of paper for each calendar month, a calendar pattern, scraps of fabric, paper, crayons, markers and cotton balls. Arrange the pieces in a picture for each month and glue. When finished, punch two holes in the top and put a ribbon through to hang.

Dream Vacation Scrapbook

Cut two pieces of lightweight cardboard 10" x 5". Reproduce boy or girl pattern large enough to fit on front of cover for each child. Color and glue to cover. Add child's name to cover. Give each child five envelopes and one copy each of the plane, sunshine, train, auto and ship to color and glue one to each envelope. Punch two holes 1" in from both corners on the left-hand sides of the envelopes. Mark matching holes on the covers and punch out. Tie everything together using string or ribbon. Let children cut pictures from magazines or provide pictures of planes, trains, autos, ships or fun things to do on sunshiny days. The child then places these in appropriate envelopes.

Soaring Plane

Pretend you are in a soaring plane on vacation. To make this flashy plane, you will need a cardboard toilet tissue tube, tape, string and aluminum foil. Enlarge the plane pattern big enough to cover the cardboard tube from end to end. Color and glue the plane to the side of the tube. Next cut long thin strips of aluminum foil and tape to end of plane, inside tube. (See illustration.) Punch a small hole in front of tube and tie on a 12" string. Now you are ready to fly. If a cardboard tube is not available, form a tube shape from construction paper and secure with tape.

Copyright © 1990, Good Apple, Inc.

140

GA1141